NEIL ARMSTRONG

AND TRAVELING TO THE MOON

DATE DUE

Edited by Clare Lewis and Abby Colich
Designed by Steve Mead and Justin Hoffman
Original illustrations © Capstone Global Library Ltd. 2015
Illustrated by Justin Hoffman
Picture research by Svetlana Zhurkin
Production by Victoria Fitzgerald
Originated by Capstone Global Library Ltd.
Printed and bound in China by CTPS

19 18 17 16 15
10 9 8 7 6 5 4 3 2 1

Library of Congress Cataloging-in-Publication Data
Hubbard, Ben, 1973- author.
  Neil Armstrong and traveling to the moon / Ben Hubbard.
      pages cm.—(Adventures in space)
  Includes bibliographical references and index.
  ISBN 978-1-4846-2515-6 (hb)—ISBN 978-1-4846-2520-0 (pb)—ISBN 978-1-4846-2530-9 (ebook) 1.
Armstrong, Neil, 1930-2012—Juvenile literature. 2. Project Apollo (U.S.)—Juvenile literature. 3. Apollo
11 (Spacecraft)—Juvenile literature. 4. Astronauts—United States—Biography—Juvenile literature. 5.
Space flight to the moon—Juvenile literature. I. Title.
  TL789.85.A75H83 2016
  629.45'0092—dc23   2015000266

[B]

This book has been officially leveled using the F&P Text Level Gradient™ Levelling System.

Acknowledgments
We would like to thank the following for permission to reproduce photographs:
Alamy: RIA Novosti, 9, The Print Collector, 4; Courtesy of the Ohio History Connection, 7; NASA, cover
(top, bottom left), 5, 8, 10, 11, 12, 13, 14, 15, 19, 20, 22–23, 26, 30, 31, 33, 34, 35, 36, 37, 38, 39, 40,
43; Shutterstock: Quaoar, cover (bottom right); University of Cincinnati: Peggy Palange, 41; Wikimedia:
Eberhard Marx, 21

We would like to thank Dr. Geza Gyuk for his invaluable help in the preparation of this book.

007333CTPSF15

CONTENTS

All words in bold, **like this**, appear in the glossary on page 45.

DREAMING OF THE MOON

On July 20, 1969, American **astronaut** Neil Armstrong paused on the bottom rung of his Lunar Module ladder and looked down. "The surface appears to be very, very fine grained as you get close to it; it's almost like a powder," he reported over his helmet radio.

Then, as around 600 million people watched from their television sets on Earth, Armstrong lowered his left foot onto the Moon's surface. He had just become the first human in history to step onto another world. His following words would be forever printed in the history books beside his name: "That's one small step for a man, one giant leap for mankind."

Lunar stories

Before scientists began working to get astronauts into space, **science fiction** writers made up stories about people being towed to the Moon by geese or flown aboard hot-air balloons. In his 1865 book, *From the Earth to the Moon*, Jules Verne described three men traveling to the Moon on a rocket. This was a remarkable prediction of the *Apollo 11* Moon mission that took place 84 years later.

TOP PLACE IN SPACE

Sending three astronauts to the Moon aboard *Apollo 11* was one of humanity's greatest accomplishments. However, just 12 years earlier, the United States did not even have the technology to launch a **rocket** into space. At that time, it was losing a race to space against its rival, the **Soviet Union**. Only an ambitious plan like a Moon landing would get the United States on top. All it had to do was design and build the spacecraft and train astronauts to fly in them. Neil Armstrong became the most famous of these astronauts.

Edwin "Buzz" Aldrin is shown stepping onto the Moon to join Neil Armstrong, who is taking the photograph.

EARLY FLYER

Neil Alden Armstrong was born in the small town of Wapakoneta, Ohio, on August 5, 1930. He first became fascinated with flying at two years old. This was when his father took him to an airshow in Cleveland, Ohio. Armstrong spent his childhood building model planes and working after school to pay for flying lessons.

After graduating from high school, Armstrong studied **aeronautical** engineering at Purdue University. He then flew fighter jets for the U.S. Navy in the Korean War. During one mission, Armstrong had to eject from his jet after being hit by enemy fire from the ground. It was the first of several near misses that Armstrong would experience during his career.

TEST PILOT

In 1955, Armstrong became a research pilot for the National Advisory Committee for Aeronautics (NACA). He tested helicopters, gliders, and over 200 different models of high-speed aircraft. One such aircraft was the rocket-powered X-15 jet, which could fly at 4,520 miles (7,274 kilometers) per hour. In 1958, NACA turned into the National Aeronautics and Space Administration (NASA)—the agency that would send Armstrong to the Moon.

SPACE Q AND A

Q. What does NASA do?

A. NASA is the U.S. agency responsible for science and technology related to air and space.

A young Neil Armstrong is dressed in his marching band uniform.

Mad for model planes

Armstrong loved designing and building model planes as a child because it taught him about the science of **aviation**. He was always more interested in reading model aircraft magazines than in the science fiction comics that many American boys enjoyed in the 1950s.

SENDING MEN TO THE MOON

While Armstrong tested rocket-powered aircraft on Earth, the Soviet Union sent the first rocket into space. The 1957 launch of the Soviet **satellite** *Sputnik 1* stunned the Americans. It meant the Soviets had the technology to fire a long-range missile into the United States. This triggered the competition between the two nations that became known as the Space Race. In 1958, the Americans launched their own satellite, *Explorer 1*, into space. The Soviets responded in 1961 by sending the first man into space: Yuri Gagarin, aboard *Vostok 1*. This news was a terrible blow for the U.S. space program. Once again, the Soviets had trumped the Americans.

■ **Ham's spacecraft missed its splashdown point in the ocean and nearly sank before the chimpanzee could be rescued.**

Animal astronaut

The first U.S. astronaut sent into space was not a man, but a chimpanzee. Ham was trained to pull a few simple levers aboard a Mercury spacecraft and was then launched into sub-orbit on January 31, 1961. Ham returned unharmed to Earth 16 minutes later.

■ The Soviet Union's *Vostok 1* blasts off from the Baikonur **Cosmodrome.**

KENNEDY'S SPACE CHALLENGE

A few weeks after *Vostok 1*, the United States launched astronaut Alan Shepard into **sub-orbit** for 15 minutes. This was only a small accomplishment compared to *Vostok 1*, which had **orbited** Earth. However, in May 1961, U.S. President John F. Kennedy announced the most ambitious space plan yet: "This nation should commit itself to achieving the goal, before the decade is out, of landing a man on the Moon and returning him safely to the Earth."

Kennedy's speech shocked the scientists at NASA. They had only just sent an astronaut into space. Now, they had under nine years to get men to the Moon and back again.

ASTRONAUT ARMSTRONG

In 1962, Armstrong applied to join NASA's space program. At that time, NASA was busy sending men into Earth's orbit on board its Mercury spacecraft. Now, it was recruiting astronauts for a new type of mission. Armstrong was a perfect match. After being accepted into the program, he joined 31 astronaut trainees to undergo advanced tests. During these tests, Armstrong had to keep his foot in a bucket of ice water and had ice water squirted into his ear.

An even harder test was being shut inside an isolation chamber. "There was no sound, no light, and no smell. They told you to come out after two hours," Armstrong said. To calculate two hours, Armstrong sang a song over and over again until he thought the time had passed. While this was difficult, the hardest challenge was to follow.

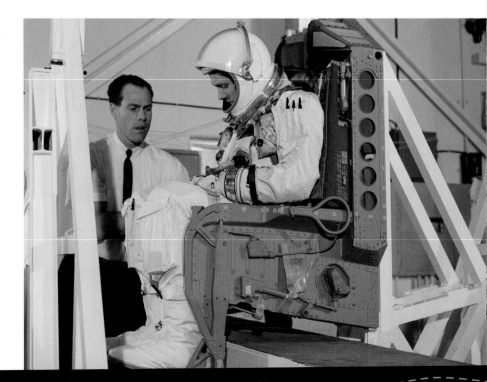

■ Neil Armstrong took part in weight and balance tests as part of his preparation for space.

Astronaut John Glenn enters *Friendship 7* to begin the first manned U.S. flight around Earth.

KEEPING COOL IN THE HEAT

For his next test, Armstrong was put into a room where the temperature reached 145 degrees Fahrenheit (63 degrees Celsius). He was then observed to see how he would cope with the extreme heat. Armstrong decided to slow his body down so it would not generate any extra heat. He sat quietly in a corner and did not move. "I don't know how well I did, but I was able to stand it in there," Armstrong said.

Mercury rising

On February 20, 1962, John Glenn became the first American astronaut to orbit Earth, aboard Mercury's *Friendship 7*. Nearly a year after *Vostok 1*, the United States had caught up with its Soviet rivals.

THE NEW NINE

Soon after becoming an astronaut trainee, Armstrong learned he would be one of the "New Nine." They were nine men who would pilot the Gemini missions. As a result of the success of the Mercury missions, Gemini was designed to practice spacewalking and spacecraft **docking**. These were essential to the U.S. plans to send a man to the Moon. To do so, two spacecraft would have to meet up and join together, or "dock," in space. Gemini was NASA's biggest and boldest program to date. It was bound to be dangerous for the New Nine.

A walk in space

New Nine astronaut Ed White made the first U.S. spacewalk aboard *Gemini 4* on June 3, 1965. White was attached to the spacecraft by a cord and used a handheld "jet gun" to move himself through space. The spacewalk lasted 23 minutes.

■ "I'm coming back in…and it's the saddest moment of my life," said Edward White before ending the first U.S. spacewalk.

SPACE SPEAK

Spacewalking: Also known as an Extra Vehicular Activity, this is when an astronaut leaves his or her spacecraft and moves around in space.

■ An astronaut sat in a cockpit at one end of this centrifuge machine, the NASA Ames 5 Degrees of Motion Simulator.

BASIC TRAINING

While the Gemini spacecraft were being built, the New Nine were put through basic astronaut training. This included parachute jumps and rides on the dreaded **centrifuge machine**. This machine spun an astronaut around at high speed so he could experience the high **g-force**, or "g's," felt during liftoff. In total, Armstrong spent five hours on the centrifuge machine and was subject to a high 15 g's.

Voskhod 2

The Soviet Union beat the United States to carry out the first spacewalk in March 1965. However, the spacewalk almost ended in disaster when **cosmonaut** Aleksey Leonov's overinflated space suit nearly prevented him from re-entering his Voskhod 2 spacecraft.

GEMINI 8

The *Gemini 8* mission was the United States' first attempt to dock a spacecraft with an unmanned rocket in space. Therefore, NASA needed its most experienced pilot, Neil Armstrong, on board. The unmanned rocket—called an Agena Target Vehicle (ATV)—lifted off from Kennedy Space Center on March 16, 1966. *Gemini 8*, carrying Armstrong and astronaut David R. Scott, followed 100 minutes later. After six hours, *Gemini 8* caught up to the ATV and successfully docked with it. Now the two spacecraft were flying in space together as one. Then, suddenly, radio contact with *Gemini 8* was lost. When contact was regained 21 minutes later, there were chilling words from the spacecraft: "We have a serious problem here…we're tumbling end over end up here."

The Cape

The Kennedy Space Center was built in 1950 on Cape Canaveral, in Florida. Today, the center features launchpads, runways, command centers, spacecraft hangers, and a seaport.

■ **This photograph shows the Agena Target Vehicle taken from *Gemini 8*, which is around 210 feet (64 meters) away.**

■ *Gemini 8* is retrieved from the ocean after its aborted mission. An inflatable flotation collar keeps the spacecraft steady.

ARMSTRONG ABORTS

Shortly after docking with the ATV, a jammed thruster on *Gemini 8* had sent both spacecraft into a spin. Armstrong immediately separated *Gemini 8* from the ATV, but the spinning continued. "It was obvious that the problem was not the Agena's. It was ours," Armstrong said.

Worse still, the spinning made Armstrong's vision blurry, and he was in danger of passing out. There was only one option: to shut down *Gemini 8*'s thrusters and fire its re-entry rockets to stabilize the spacecraft. The plan worked, but it also meant aborting the mission early. Only 10 hours after it had launched, *Gemini 8* made an emergency splashdown in the Pacific Ocean.

THE APOLLO PROGRAM

Despite Armstrong's aborted mission, the Gemini program was generally a great success for the United States. Now, Gemini was replaced by the program that would send people to the Moon: Apollo. Time, however, was in short supply. In 1966, Armstrong went on a publicity tour to South America. Meanwhile, scientists and designers at NASA worked around the clock to meet President Kennedy's 1969 deadline. Flying men the 237,700 miles (382,500 kilometers) to the Moon would require the most powerful rocket ever built: *Saturn V*.

SATURN STAGES

The *Saturn V* rocket was made up of three smaller rockets, called stages, that fit one on top of the other. Each stage was designed to fire *Saturn V* a little farther into space and then fall away when its fuel was finished.

- Stage 1 would fire for two and a half minutes, boosting *Saturn* to 42 miles (68 kilometers) above Earth.
- Stage 2 would fire for six minutes, boosting *Saturn* to 114 miles (183 kilometers) above Earth.
- Stage 3 would fire the Apollo spacecraft to a speed of 7 miles (11 kilometers) per second. This is enough speed for *Saturn* to leave Earth's orbit and start heading toward the Moon. Sitting above the third stage was the Apollo spacecraft.

SPACE Q AND A

Q. Why the Moon?

A. President Kennedy was sure sending men to another world would prove that the United States was superior to the Soviet Union in space. Kennedy's advisers told him the Moon was the most achievable destination.

Saturn V stats

Height (including spacecraft):
363 feet (111 meters)

Weight at launch:
6.2 million pounds
(2.8 million kilograms)

Total fuel:
About 800,000 gallons
(3.6 million liters)

Thrust (force to move forward):
7.5 million pounds
(3.6 million kilograms)

Apollo spacecraft

Lunar Module

exhaust nozzles

rocket engines

Stage 3

Stage 2

Stage 1

Only the Apollo spacecraft and Lunar Module would reach the Moon after the three *Saturn V* stages burned through their fuel and fell away.

APOLLO TRAGEDIES

In 1967, the United States suffered its first great space tragedy. On January 27, astronauts Virgil Grissom, Ed White, and Roger Chaffee were killed during testing of *Apollo 1*'s Command Module (CM). *Apollo 1* was scheduled to become the first manned Apollo mission into space only a few weeks later. The accident took place during a routine practice run of *Apollo 1*'s launch. The three astronauts had boarded the CM and its hatch was bolted on behind them. The countdown was then delayed because of problems with the oxygen supply and radio equipment. Suddenly, a chilling cry came over the radio: "We've got a fire in the cockpit!"

NO WAY OUT

As a flash fire swept through the CM, the astronauts struggled to open the hatch to get out. From the outside of the CM, the ground crew managed to withstand the intense heat to unbolt the hatch in just a few minutes. But they were too late—the astronauts inside were dead. A report on the accident later found that some safety features may have been overlooked. NASA was in such a hurry to get a man onto the Moon that it had not given enough attention to crew safety. The Apollo program had faced disaster before it had even gotten off the ground.

Cosmonaut killed

The Soviet Union also suffered from a cosmonaut death in 1967. Vladimir Komarov crashed to Earth after the parachute on his *Soyuz 1* spacecraft failed. Many decades later, it emerged that around 124 people had also died during a 1960 explosion at the Soviet Baikonur Cosmodrome. The Soviets made sure this "Nedelin Catastrophe" was kept secret at the time.

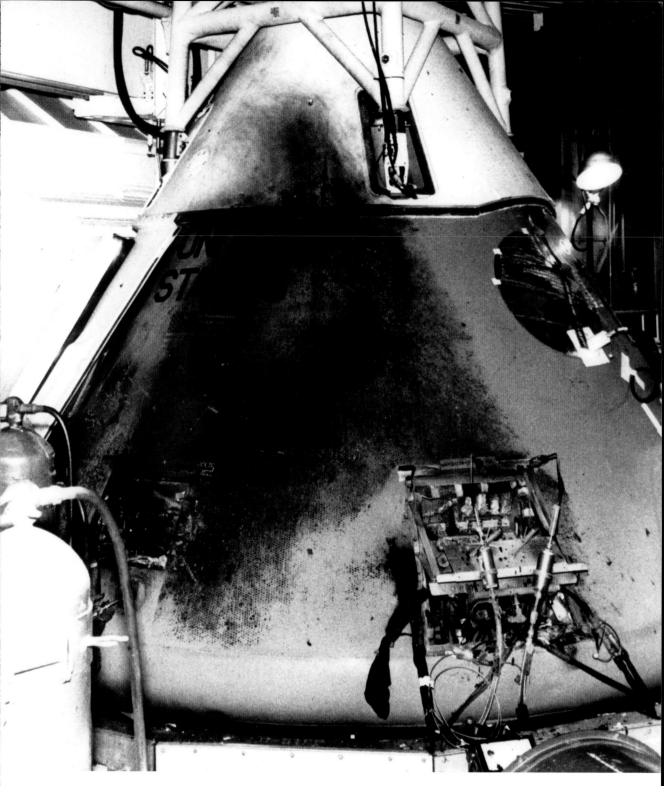

■ Scorch marks from the intense heat can be seen after the tragedy on *Apollo 1*. Unlike later spacecraft, the Command Module's hatch was not fitted with explosive bolts.

TRAINING FOR THE MOON

Three days after NASA released its report on the *Apollo 1* tragedy, Armstrong and 17 other astronauts were told they had made the final short list for the Moon mission. Armstrong said this put him into an "unspoken competition in which the prize was the ultimate flight test, the first lunar landing."

Gravity training for the Moon began immediately. On the Moon, there is only one-sixth of the amount of gravity there is on Earth. In space, astronauts do not feel the effects of gravity because they are actually constantly falling. To imitate the low-gravity conditions of the Moon, the astronauts practiced walking in their space suits in a swimming pool. To practice being **weightless** in space, the astronauts trained aboard a reduced-gravity aircraft. Because the weightless conditions often made the astronauts **nauseous**, the aircraft was nicknamed the "vomit comet."

■ Training in the "Flying Bedstead" gave Armstrong the essential practice needed to land the Lunar Module on the Moon.

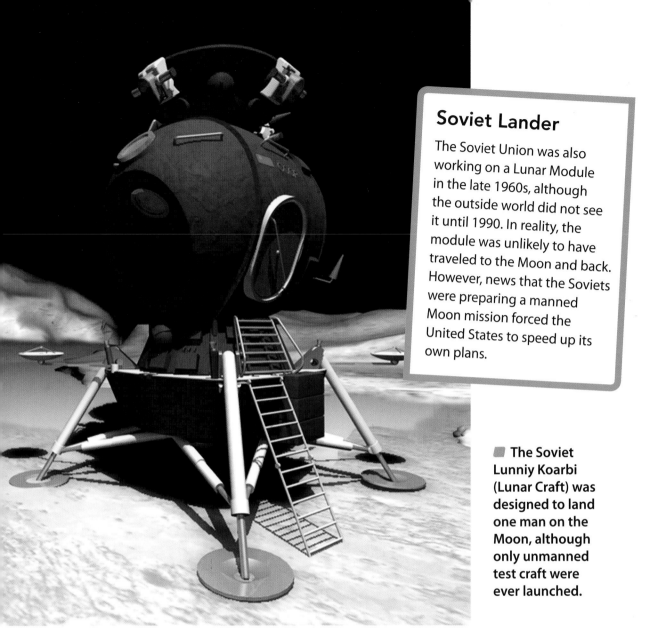

Soviet Lander

The Soviet Union was also working on a Lunar Module in the late 1960s, although the outside world did not see it until 1990. In reality, the module was unlikely to have traveled to the Moon and back. However, news that the Soviets were preparing a manned Moon mission forced the United States to speed up its own plans.

▩ The Soviet Lunniy Koarbi (Lunar Craft) was designed to land one man on the Moon, although only unmanned test craft were ever launched.

LUNAR LANDER

The astronauts also trained aboard the "Flying Bedstead," a practice model of the Lunar Module that would land on the Moon's surface. During his training flight, Armstrong had another near miss when the "Flying Bedstead" spun out of control in the air. He was able to eject at the last minute, before the module crashed and exploded into flames.

APOLLO 8

With fears that the Soviet Union was planning a lunar landing, the United States stepped up its efforts to launch its mission to the Moon. *Apollo 8* would not land on the Moon. Instead, it would circle around it, take photos of its far side (the side of the Moon we can't see from Earth), and fly back to Earth. Although Armstrong was not aboard *Apollo 8*, he was told he would be commander of *Apollo 11*, the first mission to actually land men on the Moon. The countdown to *Apollo 8* began. From "T minus four days and counting," Apollo's 5,000 mission personnel were on high alert, as 60 television cameras beamed pictures of the spacecraft's approaching launch around the world.

TV missions

Unlike the Soviet space program, the United States caught every moment of its space missions on camera. On Christmas Eve, 1968, the *Apollo 8* astronauts issued a message of goodwill that was broadcast live to hundreds of millions of television viewers across the globe.

■ Photographs taken from *Apollo 8* gave people at home a never-before-seen view of Earth's isolated position in space.

EARTHRISE

On December 21, 1968, *Apollo 8* blasted into space. After orbiting Earth once, *Apollo 8*'s rockets fired it to an "escape **velocity**" of 25,000 miles (40,000 kilometers) per hour to send it to the Moon. Less than three days later, *Apollo 8*'s rockets fired again to put it into the Moon's orbit. People at NASA held their breath as *Apollo 8* traveled around the Moon to its far side—a place never seen by human eyes. Then, to everyone's relief, *Apollo 8* emerged on the other side. The astronauts on board then glimpsed something never seen before by humans: Earth rising above the Moon's horizon.

SPACE Q AND A

Q. What does "T minus," or "T-," mean?

A. "T minus" means the time remaining before a rocket's liftoff.

Focus on:

APOLLO 11 SPACECRAFT

By mid-1969, NASA was making its finishing touches to the *Apollo 11* spacecraft that would take Neil Armstrong, Buzz Aldrin, and Michael Collins to the Moon. The spacecraft sat on top of the *Saturn V* rocket and was made up of three main parts: the Command Module (CM), the Service Module (SM), and the Lunar Module (LM).

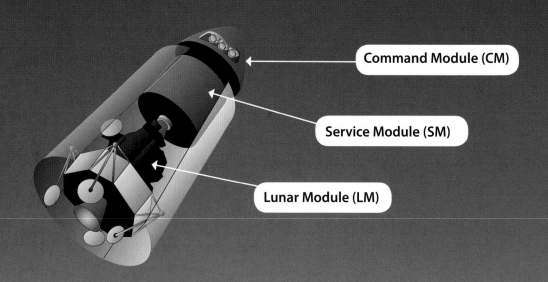

Command Module (CM)

Service Module (SM)

Lunar Module (LM)

Although tucked away beneath the Command and Service Modules at launch, the Lunar Module would be unpacked in space before its descent to the Moon.

Command Module controls

The Command Module's control panels were positioned in front of the astronauts' seats. Primitive by today's standards, the panels consisted of hundreds of switches, lights, and simple displays. Altogether, the Command Module had less computing power than a modern cell phone.

Lunar Module

The *Apollo 11* Lunar Module was made up of two parts: a **descent** stage at the bottom and an **ascent** stage at the top. The descent stage was fitted with a small engine, four legs, and footpads to land on the Moon, and the equipment that would be used on its surface. The ascent stage was where the astronauts worked and slept. When they had finished their mission, the astronauts would blast off from the Moon in the ascent stage, leaving the descent stage behind. The ascent stage would then re-dock with the CM and SM, which stayed in the Moon's orbit.

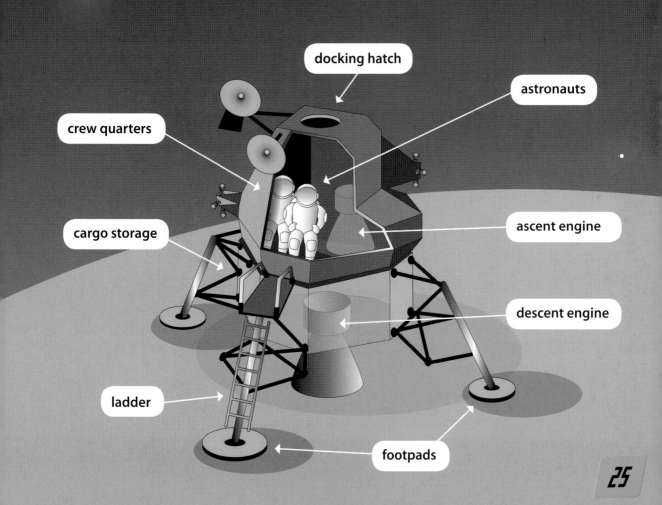

docking hatch

astronauts

crew quarters

cargo storage

ascent engine

descent engine

ladder

footpads

COUNTDOWN BEGINS

With 28 hours to go before the launch of *Apollo 11*, the official countdown began. This was the last chance for the mission controllers to make their final checks. Radio communications, Earth's **tracking stations**, emergency abort systems, and weather conditions all had to be checked alongside the Saturn rocket and *Apollo 11* spacecraft.

■ **The swing arms move away from *Apollo 11* and its *Saturn V* rocket as flames below signal its liftoff.**

COUNTDOWN

T–28 hours
System checks start as the countdown begins.

T–9 hours
Fuel is loaded into *Saturn V*.

T–5 hours, 2 minutes
The three astronauts, Armstrong, Aldrin, and Collins, are examined by a doctor.

T–4 hours, 32 minutes
The astronauts eat a final breakfast of coffee, orange juice, scrambled eggs, toast, and steak. Hundreds of thousands of people gather at Cape Canaveral to watch the launch.

T–3 hours, 57 minutes
The astronauts are helped into their space suits. From that point on, they do not breathe fresh air again until returning from the Moon eight days later.

T–2 hours, 55 minutes
The astronauts arrive at the launchpad.

T–2 hours, 40 minutes
The astronauts board the Command Module of *Apollo 11*. Armstrong settles into the commander's seat and wonders whether the launch will go ahead: "These things were canceled more often than they were launched. We'd go in, climb out, go back, and get ready for another day," he said.

T–15 minutes
Final checks are completed and the Command Module switches to internal power.

T–9 seconds
White clouds billow around the rocket's base as the engine ignition begins. In the launch control center, a button saying "LAUNCH COMMIT" is pressed. Fire blasts from the bottom of *Apollo 11* and a deafening boom fills the air.

T–0 seconds
A voice from the control center calls out: "We have liftoff! We have liftoff!"

LIFTOFF

As *Apollo 11* blasted into space, the rocket's engines sent out a thunderous roar and shook the astronauts violently in their seats. "In that first 30 seconds it was very hard to hear anything over the radio—even inside the helmet with the headphones," Armstrong said.

After *Apollo 11*'s first and second stages fell away, the conditions slowly became bearable. As the spacecraft entered Earth's orbit, the astronauts got used to working, eating, and sleeping in their temporary home. For the three days it took to get to the Moon, the astronauts followed a busy schedule. They prepared the Lunar Module, sent back television broadcasts to Earth, and checked their instruments to make sure they were on course.

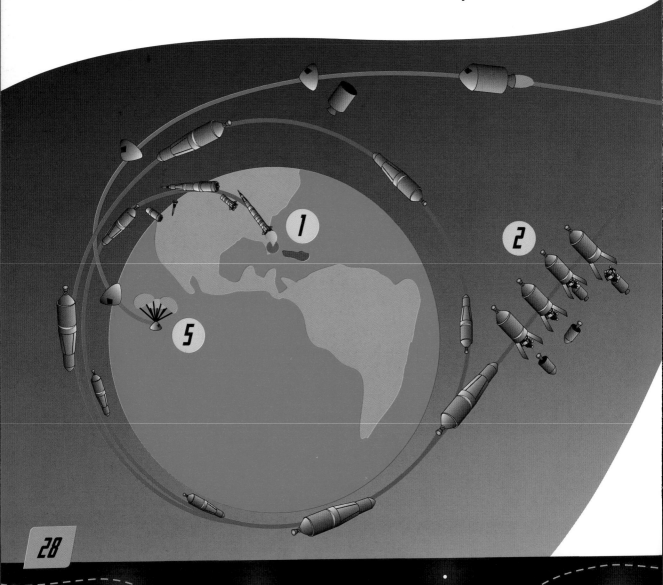

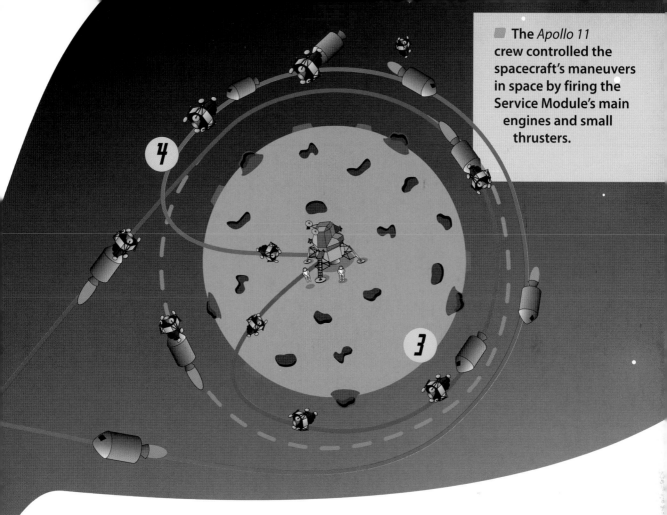

The *Apollo 11* crew controlled the spacecraft's maneuvers in space by firing the Service Module's main engines and small thrusters.

1 *Apollo 11* lifts off, orbits the Earth 1.5 times, and discards the first two stages of the *Saturn V* rocket. The third stage fires *Apollo 11* toward the Moon.

2 The Command Module (CM) and Service Module (SM) detaches from *Saturn*'s third stage, turns around, and pulls out the Lunar Module from inside the third stage. The third stage falls away.

3 *Apollo 11* orbits the Moon. Armstrong and Aldrin detach in the Lunar Module, called *Eagle*, and land on the Moon. The CM and SM stay in orbit.

4 The Lunar Module's ascent stage launches from the Moon, re-docks with the Command Module, and is discarded.

5 The CM and SM blast back toward Earth. The CM separates from the SM and splashes down into the Pacific Ocean.

THERE AND BACK

The *Apollo 11* spacecraft had to perform a series of maneuvers to get the astronauts to the Moon and back again. Each maneuver had to be timed perfectly, since there was not enough fuel to make mistakes.

MOON LANDING

With well over half a billion television viewers watching the Moon landing, it was important that nothing went wrong. However, as Armstrong flew the *Eagle* Lunar Module toward the surface, an alarm sounded from its computer. Mission Control in Houston, Texas, told Armstrong to ignore the alarm, but he knew something was not right. *Eagle* had flown past its planned landing spot and was heading for a field of boulders. Worse still, *Eagle*'s fuel gauge had dropped dangerously low, and Mission Control warned that *Eagle* had only 60 seconds of fuel left to land. "Thirty seconds," Mission Control called out soon after.

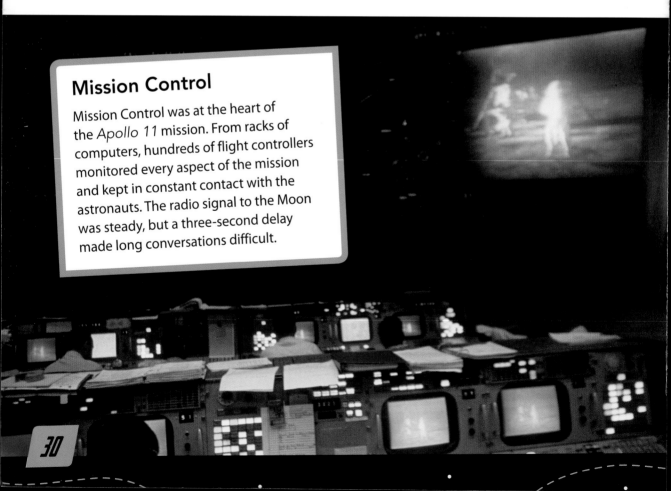

Mission Control

Mission Control was at the heart of the *Apollo 11* mission. From racks of computers, hundreds of flight controllers monitored every aspect of the mission and kept in constant contact with the astronauts. The radio signal to the Moon was steady, but a three-second delay made long conversations difficult.

■ **Buzz Aldrin is pictured with a Solar Wind Composition experiment, shown to his right.**

DIFFICULT DESCENT

Armstrong was NASA's most experienced pilot, but he was worried—his heart rate had jumped to a rapid 156 beats per minute. Silence fell over Mission Control as everyone held their breath. At the last possible moment, Armstrong saw a landing spot—a clearing beside a small crater. As he maneuvered downward, *Eagle* kicked up gray Moon dust, making it impossible to see the ground. Then, **sensors** on *Eagle*'s footpads detected the surface, and Armstrong let all four pads touch the lunar ground. Seconds later, Mission Control broke into cheers as Armstrong's voice came over the radio: "The *Eagle* has landed."

Focus on:

WALKING ON THE MOON

When Armstrong stepped from *Eagle* onto the Moon's surface, he united the people watching from Earth in admiration. The Moon, however, was a cold, lonely place with no sign of life. Armstrong's first "small step for a man" was into soft, gray Moon dust. "The surface is fine and powdery. I can kick it up loosely with my toe," Armstrong said. Because there is no air or wind on the Moon to blow the dust and soil away, it lay like a blanket over everything.

To breathe outside their *Eagle* Lunar Module, Armstrong and Aldrin had to wear space suits. These provided the astronauts with the vital life support systems they needed to survive in the lunar environment.

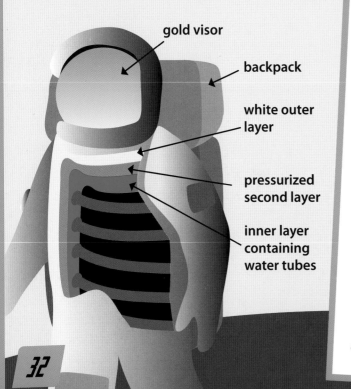

gold visor

backpack

white outer layer

pressurized second layer

inner layer containing water tubes

Space suits

The *Apollo 11* space suit was like a small spacecraft that protected the astronaut inside. An inner layer contained water tubes to keep the astronaut cool, and a pressurized second layer formed an airtight seal against space. A white outer layer protected against solar radiation and **micro-meteoroids**. A backpack provided oxygen, controlled the space suit's temperature, and contained radio communications. A gold visor on the helmet shielded against harsh ultraviolet light from the Sun. On Earth, the bulky space suits weighed 180 pounds (81 kilograms), but because of the Moon's low gravity, the astronauts could easily jump around in them.

Armstrong was the first human to make a footprint on the Moon. Because there is no rain or wind on the Moon, it could remain there for millions of years.

Extreme Moon

Because there is little **atmosphere** on the Moon, it suffers from extreme temperatures. The daytime temperature can reach 250 degrees Fahrenheit (121 degrees Celsius), and at night it can drop to -250 degrees Fahrenheit (-156 degrees Celsius). The Moon has no air to transmit sound, so it is a completely silent world.

MOON TASKS

After stepping onto the Moon's surface, Armstrong's first task was to collect a rock sample, in case they had to leave in a hurry. The rock would provide **geologists** on Earth with important information about the Moon, such as possible signs of life or water. Armstrong and Aldrin then set up equipment to conduct experiments that would be monitored from Earth. One of the experiments measured "Moonquakes" and provided information about the Moon's structure. Another reflected back laser beams from Earth to calculate Earth's exact distance from the Moon.

▉ **Armstrong found that the best way to take photographs, such as this one of Aldrin, was to mount the camera onto a bracket on the front of his space suit.**

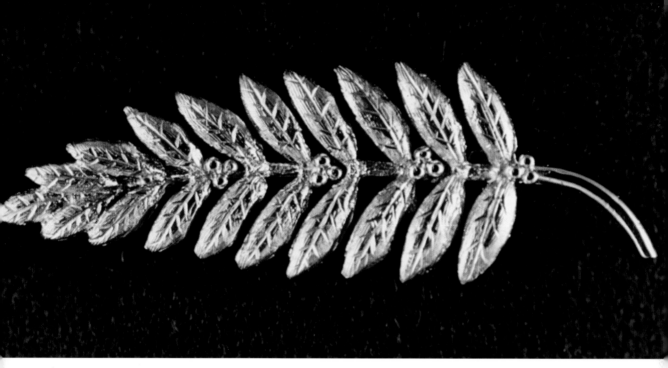

■ Among the plaques and medals the Apollo astronauts left on the Moon was this gold olive branch, meant as a symbol of peace.

Flags and plaques

The astronauts unveiled a plaque commemorating their mission and planted a U.S. flag on the Moon. The flag was designed with a horizontal pole so it looked like it was flapping in the breeze. Armstrong also left a packet of medals in honor of the deceased *Apollo 1* astronauts and the Soviet cosmonauts Vladimir Komarov and Yuri Gagarin.

CAUGHT ON CAMERA

The astronauts had strict instructions to catch their whole Moon expedition on camera. They used black and white television cameras to transmit footage back to Earth. They had photographic cameras to take pictures of themselves and their surroundings. Aldrin took only one photograph of Armstrong, showing his back. The only time his image was captured clearly was when it was reflected in the visor of Buzz Aldrin's helmet. "I don't think Buzz had any reason to take my picture, and it never occurred to me that he should. I have always said Buzz was the far more photogenic of the crew," Armstrong said.

EARTH BOUND

After only two hours and 31 minutes on the Moon's surface, Armstrong and Aldrin climbed back aboard *Eagle*. Their mission over, the astronauts had to prepare for the voyage home. Once back inside *Eagle*, they changed out of their space suits and ate a meal. However, the gray Moon dust had gotten into everything and made the air smell like wet ash. The astronauts had to once again put on their space suits to throw away anything they didn't need. Dust-covered space boots, empty food packages, and small bags of human waste were thrown out from *Eagle*, creating the first lunar litter.

After the astronauts had a short nap, *Eagle*'s ascent stage blasted off from the Moon to dock with Collins in the Command and Service Module. Collins had been alone for some of the time with no radio contact while Armstrong and Aldrin were on the Moon. Now, as Collins helped his dusty colleagues back into the module, Armstrong passed him the precious cargo of Moon rock and soil.

■ **Buzz Aldrin shows the TV audience on Earth how to make a sandwich in space. At this time, the Apollo spacecraft was around 137,000 miles (220,000 kilometers) from Earth.**

Space food

Astronaut food was pre-cooked, freeze-dried, and packaged in meal-sized airtight bags or tubes. Some of the meals were ready to eat and others required hot water. In weightless space, it was important that no crumbs or liquid floated from a food bag and interfered with the equipment. Therefore, the meals included chocolate pudding and beef and vegetable paste.

Armstrong rests inside the Lunar Module following his Moon walk.

SPACE Q AND A

Q. How did the astronauts use the toilet on the Moon?

A. The *Apollo 11* space suit had a type of special built-in toilet bag called a "Maximum Absorbency Garment." This collected and stored human waste to be discarded later.

SPLASHDOWN

After nearly three days of traveling through space, *Apollo 11* neared Earth. Landing, however, was as dangerous as liftoff. After separating from the Service Module, the Command Module hit Earth's atmosphere at a whopping 25,000 miles (40,000 kilometers) per hour. As the module tore through the clouds, its orange and white parachutes flapped open. The parachutes stabilized the module, but as it hit the Pacific Ocean hard, each astronaut let out a loud grunt. After bobbing around in the rough water, U.S. Navy divers helped the astronauts from Apollo's hatch into rescue rafts. Their mission was complete.

■ **U.S. President Richard Nixon visits the *Apollo 11* astronauts in their quarantine trailer.**

■ The people of New York City line the streets to welcome home the *Apollo 11* astronauts in one of the largest parades in the city's history.

MOON GERMS

Nobody was sure if the astronauts had been exposed to any dangerous germs on the Moon that could harm people on Earth. So, the astronauts were put into a quarantine trailer for 16 days. Inside, a phone enabled the astronauts to speak to their families. One of Armstrong's first calls was to his mother: "Hello, Mom, this is Neil...all three of us are just fine...none of us got sick and all of the machinery worked. It was fantastically beautiful. The surface is covered with a black dust, and it got all over our nice, clean white suits and wouldn't brush off."

World celebration

After being given a clean bill of health, the astronauts left the quarantine trailer to a new life as world celebrities. They embarked on a 45-day "Giant Leap" tour around the world, which included state dinners, TV interviews, and ticker-tape parades. However, like cosmonaut Yuri Gagarin who came before them, the Apollo astronauts often found their newfound fame difficult to handle.

LIFE AFTER APOLLO

The U.S. Moon missions did not end with *Apollo 11*. Between 1969 and 1972, five more Apollo spacecraft landed on the Moon. Ten more astronauts walked on the lunar surface. Neil Armstrong, however, was not among them. Instead, Armstrong was expected to be the American poster boy for space. This meant many official dinners and talking engagements in the United States and abroad. Armstrong even traveled to Russia to meet the first woman in space, Valentina Tereshkova, and Yuri Gagarin's widow. Armstrong told Valentina Gagarina he had left a medal honoring her husband on the Moon.

Armstrong was awarded the first Congressional Space Medal of Honor.

Apollo 13

In 1970, the U.S. space program was shaken when *Apollo 13* had to abort its mission to the Moon. The spacecraft was damaged by an explosion in its oxygen tank 200,000 miles (320,000 kilometers) from Earth. The crew only just made it home alive by using the air on board the spacecraft's Lunar Module.

■ Armstrong explains the science of spaceflight to engineering students in 1974.

AFTER NASA

Armstrong was something of a reluctant celebrity and retired from NASA in 1971. His fascination with aviation had started with the model aircraft magazines he had read as a boy. After NASA, Armstrong decided to use his knowledge to teach aerospace engineering at the University of Cincinnati, in Ohio. He later worked as a spokesman for several businesses and as a spaceflight accident investigator. Armstrong's fame never let him stray far from public view, but he didn't like to profit from his celebrity status. He hired a full-time secretary to help answer his many letters, but stopped sending autographs after some were put up for sale on eBay. Armstrong also made his barber pay $3,000 to charity after he sold a lock of his hair. In 2012, Neil Armstrong died after a heart operation. He was 82 years old.

MISSION ACCOMPLISHED?

In 1969, *Apollo 11* completed President Kennedy's dream of "landing a man on the Moon before the decade is out." The mission had been designed to beat the Soviet Union in space. However, after this had been achieved, it was unclear what the next challenge should be. Throughout the Apollo missions, the United States had been a nation in a state of turmoil. It was fighting an unpopular war in Vietnam, and there was great social unrest at home. Many considered the Moon missions wasteful, when people were struggling for their basic human rights on Earth. In 1972, the Apollo program was canceled, and the *Apollo 17* astronauts were the last men to walk on the Moon.

FINDING PEACE IN SPACE

The Apollo program, often called the "greatest technological achievement in human history," cost over $20 billion. However, it was anything but a waste of money. It provided enormous breakthroughs in technology, such as the development of the microchip used in all modern computing. It showed that humans are capable of traveling long distances in space and surviving on other worlds. It also paved the way for cooperation between old enemies. In 1970, the docking of the *Apollo–Soyuz* spacecrafts put an end to the Space Race, as Russians and Americans extended the hand of peace in space.

Neil Armstrong described the Earth from the Moon as "big, and bright, and beautiful." Hopefully, one legacy of future space programs is for all nations to recognize the need for peace on Earth as we continue to explore space.

The plaque left on the *Apollo 11* Lunar Module reads: "Here men from the planet Earth first set foot upon the moon July 1969, A.D. We came in peace for all mankind."

TIMELINE

August 5, 1930   Neil Armstrong is born in Wapakoneta, Ohio

1952   Armstrong becomes a research pilot for the National Advisory Committee for Aeronautics (NACA)

1955   Armstrong becomes a test pilot for NACA

1957   The Soviet Union launches the satellite *Sputnik 1* into orbit around Earth

1958   The United States launches its first satellite, *Explorer 1*

April 12, 1961   Cosmonaut Yuri Gagarin becomes the first man into space aboard *Vostok 1*

May 5, 1961   American astronaut Alan Shepard is launched into sub-orbit for 15 minutes aboard *Freedom 7*

May 25, 1961   President John F. Kennedy announces that the United States will land a man on the Moon by the end of the decade

1962   Armstrong becomes one of NASA's "New Nine" astronauts selected for the Gemini missions

February 20, 1962   John Glenn becomes the first American to orbit Earth aboard the Mercury spacecraft *Friendship 7*

March 16, 1966   Armstrong has to abort the *Gemini 8* mission when the spacecraft is put into a spin after docking with the Agena rocket

January 27, 1967   Astronauts Virgil Grissom, Ed White, and Roger Chaffee are killed during testing of *Apollo 1*

December 21, 1968   *Apollo 8* makes the first manned trip into the Moon's orbit and back

July 20, 1969   Neil Armstrong becomes the first man to step foot on the Moon, as commander of the *Apollo 11* mission

1970   The United States and the Soviet Union join forces in space. This enables the docking of the *Apollo–Soyuz* spacecrafts in 1975.

1971   Armstrong retires from NASA

1972   The last NASA astronauts land on the Moon as the Apollo program is canceled

2012   Neil Armstrong dies at 82 years old

GLOSSARY

aeronautical science that deals with airplanes and flying

ascent act of rising upward

astronaut person trained to travel into space aboard a spacecraft

atmosphere protective layer of air and other gases that surrounds Earth, allowing living things to survive

aviation flying or operating aircraft

centrifuge machine spinning machine that inflicts a high g-force on a cosmonaut or astronaut

Cosmodrome Soviet launching site for rockets and other spacecraft

cosmonaut astronaut belonging to the Russian, or former Soviet Union, space program

descent falling or moving downward

docking two spacecraft joining in space

geologist scientist who studies rocks and soil

g-force short for "gravity-force," a force of gravity, high loads of which are felt during rapid acceleration

gravity pulling force that attracts objects to one another

micro-meteoroid very small object moving in space, often made of rock

nauseous feeling like you are about to throw up

orbit curved path an object follows around a planet, or other celestial body, as a result of its gravity

rocket cylindrical object that is driven upward by burning fuel and expelling the gases to provide propulsion

satellite object that orbits a star, planet, or asteroid. Satellites can be natural, such as the Moon, or human-made, such as *Sputnik 1*.

science fiction fiction based in the future or on different worlds

sensor device that detects and records heat, sound, or movement. Sensor pads can be used in medicine to measure a person's pulse.

Soviet Union (full name, the Union of Soviet Socialist Republics, or USSR), union of Russia and 14 surrounding states, dissolved in 1991

sub-orbit path that does not complete a full orbit of Earth or another planet

tracking station place that monitors the movement of spacecraft, ships, or aircraft using radar

velocity an object's speed

weightless something that is weightless is not held down by gravity. In space, the force of gravity is not felt.

FIND OUT MORE

BOOKS

Green, Carl R. *Walking on the Moon: The Amazing Apollo 11 Mission* (American Space Missions). Berkeley Heights, N.J.: Enslow, 2013.

Morris, Neil. *What Does Space Exploration Do for Us?* (Earth, Space, and Beyond). Chicago: Raintree, 2012.

Oxlade, Chris. *The Moon* (Astronaut Travel Guides). Chicago: Raintree, 2013.

Parker, Steve. *Space Exploration* (How It Works). Broomall, PA.: Mason Crest, 2011.

DVDs

For All Mankind (2010)
This is a documentary about the Apollo program compiled from the astronauts' own footage shot during the missions.

In the Shadow of the Moon (2008)
The Apollo astronauts discuss the Moon missions in this documentary by Ron Howard.

Moonwalk One (2009)
This documentary is about the first Moon landing and *Apollo 11*, and it features interviews with its astronauts.

Stephen Hawking's Universe (2010)
The world-famous cosmologist explores the mysteries of the universe, including the Big Bang, the origins of the universe, and the search for extraterrestrial life.

PLACES TO VISIT

Kennedy Space Center, Merritt Island, Florida
www.kennedyspacecenter.com
The Kennedy Space Center features exhibits about space technology and observation decks that look down on the rocket launch sites and the launch control center.

The Museum of Science and Industry, Chicago, Illinois
www.msichicago.org
This museum features an extensive collection dedicated to the history of space exploration.